OUT OF THE CABBAGE PATCH

Florence Littauer

HARVEST HOUSE PUBLISHERS
Eugene, Oregon 97402

OUT OF THE CABBAGE PATCH

Copyright © 1984 by Harvest House Publishers
Eugene, Oregon 97402

ISBN 0-89081-454-6

Printed in the United States of America.

PREFACE

In this book Florence Littauer has taken the popularity of the Cabbage Patch Kids and brought it into her personal perspective. With her usual humor she gives reasons why the American public was ready for a doll who was unique, in need of a mother, and up for adoption. How Florence ties this fad to a moving message, including the adoption of her real-life Cabbage Patch Doll, is for you to read and discover.

CONTENTS

1

Where Is the Cabbage Patch?

I grew up in that innocent era when none of us children knew the facts of life. I remember how many days I took getting up the courage to ask my mother where my little brother James had come from.

"The stork brought him," she said quickly and left the room. I had never seen a stork, although I had glimpsed pictures of a funny white bird with a big beak carrying a bright-eyed baby along in a diaper. Somehow I was nervous about a bird being in charge of flying over tall buildings carrying my baby brother, and when mother told me we were going to have another delivery in January, I worried about how this baby would keep warm on the trip from wherever to here.

One day I expressed my concerns to my friend

Peggy. "There's no stork," she scoffed. "That's a fairy tale like Santa Claus. My mother says that she took me out of the Cabbage Patch and that I was the cutest baby there."

"Where's the Cabbage Patch?" I asked in hopes I could get there early and choose my own little brother.

Peggy hesitated only slightly before stating with assurance, "It's right outside of Boston."

That was a discouraging answer because Boston was too far away, but when my mother left one cold night to go pick out our baby, I pictured her standing in the snow choosing from among the rows of cabbages. Or did cabbages grow in clusters? I had never seen a cabbage in its natural habitat, but the Patch must have been near Boston, for it was over a week before my mother returned with little Ron.

As I grew up I put the stork and the cabbages in a box with Santa Claus, the shoemaker elves, the Easter Bunny, and the tooth fairy.

As I raised my own children, Santa Claus emerged each year along with his new helper Rudolf the Red-nosed Reindeer, and the Easter Bunny hopped out to be joined by his brother Buggs Bunny. But the fable of the Cabbage Patch stayed under cover with the stork until the autumn of 1983, when I read an ad that said, "We have the genuine Cabbage Patch Dolls—one-of-a-kind—available for adoption."

The picture showed a homely little doll who could conceivably have come right off Mr. Mc-Gregor's Cabbage Patch. Her hair was obviously made from thick yarn, her eyes were placed too close together as if looking at each other, and her mouth was pulled in as if she had just removed her false teeth. Was someone trying to market such an unfortunate child?

And yet as I gazed at her she had a certain pathetic appeal, and I knew instantly that she needed a mother.

With a mixture of disbelief and nostalgia, I wondered who had dug up the Cabbage Patch for a new generation and whether this doll could cultivate Christmas sales.

The answer to this question is a history of past inspiration, present demand, and future appreciation.

PAST INSPIRATION

In 1978 folk artist Xavier Roberts founded the original Appalachian Artworks in Cleveland, Georgia, and began to birth one-of-a-kind babies. With $5000 from supportive friends, he leased a former clinic and named it the Babyland General Hospital. Instead of selling dolls in a store, he allowed future parents to come in and chose their own baby from an assortment lying around in individual cribs, cradles, and bassinets. Salesmen wore white coats like doctors and the saleswomen dressed like nurses. Customers spoke in hushed hospital tones and there was an emotional tug as a child would find just the right doll for her. Each new mother was assured that her child was special, as each one was handmade and guaranteed to be unique.

These adoptions of traditional Appalachian folk dolls with their pudgy, chinless faces seemed to cry out for protection and love, and the clinic setting gave new parents the feeling they had done more than buy a mass-produced doll off a shelf.

Roberts added to this atmosphere by producing birth certificates with hand- and footprints and creating adoption papers for each offspring. Instead of purchasing a toy, you adopted a baby. Instead of buying a doll, you paid an adoption fee of $125. Roberts originally invented this idea to inspire children to take care of his creations, but the adopting concept became far more significant than he had imagined.

To add to the uniqueness, Roberts gave each baby a name, which he placed on each birth certificate. To help him come up with enough fresh labels, he pulled out ideas from the 1938 Georgia birth records, and he guarantees that no two dolls have the same name.

At first he called them Little People, but later, remembering how he was told as a child that babies were found in cabbage patches, he capitalized on the old myth and called them Cabbage Patch Kids. These combined strokes of merchandising genius caused Roberts' sales to jump, and Babyland General Hospital has delivered over 250,000 original babies in just five years!

When Coleco Industries of West Hartford, Connecticut, heard of the popularity of Roberts' offspring, they signed a contract to mass-produce the Cabbage Patch Kids. Although they couldn't turn every toy store into a hospital and make the clerks into nurses, they did maintain the other appealing qualities of the little tykes.

By computerizing the assembly line, Coleco was able to vary each doll enough to make them one-of-a-kind. They created numerous skin colorations, including black, and they expect to add Asian and Hispanic looks. The coarse yarn hair, with no attempt to appear real, comes in many colors, including bright orange, and the shiny eyes, set close together, come in normal shades plus Kelly green. Dimples are scattered here and there, and each sunken mouth has its own wry twist.

Coleco retained the idea of birth certificates and keeps a computer full of names busily pairing them up to avoid any duplication.

The other day I stopped a little girl on the street in Toronto; she was carrying a Cabbage Patch Doll.

"What's her name?" I asked.

"Brenda Eve, but I don't really like the name."

"Why don't you change it if you don't like it?"

"Oh, I couldn't do that!" she answered quickly. "This is the name she was born with." She sighed as a mother whose child isn't quite what she'd wanted but who would just have to grin and bear it.

In each box, along with the birth certificate, come the adoption papers, to be filled out by each new mother. By putting her signature on the dotted line she commits herself to the serious responsibilities of child-rearing. In one year Coleco birthed about 3 million babies straight out of the Cabbage Patch!

PRESENT DEMAND

Many toys come and go, but some go on forever. Every manufacturer hopes his presentation will be a hit, but there is no proven magic ingredient that spells success. Who would have dared hope that a metal coil called Slinky that did nothing smarter than fall down stairs would still be selling almost 40 years after this dubious creation? Who would ever want to buy a product so unattractively named as Silly Putty and with a function so unnecessary as pulling pictures off comic strips and causing them to disappear as you rolled the blob into a rubber ball? Yet this product, created in 1950, is still bouncing its way to eternal life.

And how about the Hula Hoop, that had 30 million

Americans going around in circles during 1958? My daughter Lauren at four years old was so adorable twirling her little hips to keep the hoop alive that I put her in the opening of *Guys and Dolls*, a show I was directing at the time. When the curtain opened on the New York street scene, there was little Lauren center stage encircled by a whirling Hula Hoop.

While not a result of her performance, the fad faded and the old plastic hoops are found today only in garage sales.

Who would be foolish enough to pay $4 for a common stone in a cardboard box? Over a million people in 1975 took home a Pet Rock to love and cherish till death did them part. They must have been taken in by this pet that didn't leak, bark, or demand attention, for they gave them to each other for Christmas presents.[1]

Yesterday I saw a young black girl in a hotel elevator. I asked her why she was wearing one earring hanging down in the shape of a large white glove. She explained that it showed she loved Michael Jackson.

"Did you lose the other one?" I asked.

"Oh, no," she said reverently. "*He* only wears one white glove and so *we* only wear one white glove. It makes us feel close to Michael."

Who knows what fad will catch on when, where, or for how long? Will it be Castle Greyskull, the Gremlins, or Go Bots?

Christmas 1983 will go down in fad history as the year of the Cabbage Patch Kids. From out of a field of Chinese Cabbage, planeloads of dolls from Hong Kong made their way to the toy stores of America. Overnight Barbie and Ken seemed too sleek and sterile, Strawberry Shortcake pulled her hat over her face in shame, Betsy-Wetsy wanted to get out of her diapers, Chatty Cathy stopped talking, and Raggedy Ann eloped with Andy. Cheerful Tearful got depressed and Baby Alive wished she were dead!

Maternal instincts popped up in females from two to 92 as droves dove through piles of boxes seeking the one little tot whose eyes would look up in need and whose arms would stretch out in love. New mothers weren't satisfied with one Patch; they wanted a Batch. Before Toys-R-Us knew what hit them, the shelves were barren and so were the potential mothers in mobs outside the stores.

As the shortage became apparent, women who didn't even know a little child became lustful for the possession of a Cabbage Patch Doll.

Newspapers headlined Cabbage Patch stories daily.

A woman broke her leg when she fell off a ladder she had climbed to reach a doll hidden on layaway for someone else.

A 75-year-old man was knocked down and trampled when the door opened and people pushed into the store in search of Kids.

A man got up at 3:30 in the morning and stood in the rain until the toy store opened.

Managers handed out numbered cards to give some sense of order to the customers, who were shoving each other into walls and knocking over display racks.

Mothers felt like failures if they couldn't get a doll for their child, who would no doubt sink into a rejection syndrome without the one toy essential to life, liberty, and the pursuit of happiness.

A group of screaming mothers mobbed the manager of a toy store as they found him at the loading dock, and against his protests they grabbed all the boxes they could carry and ran to the checkout stands.

Managers watched helplessly as several women would pull on one box, ripping it apart in a passion for possession.

One lady set two dolls on a shelf and stepped back to evaluate which one she would choose. As she watched, two other ladies grabbed the dolls and left her staring at an empty shelf.

A lady in tears pulled a Kid from another woman's arms. The victim got even by lassoing the perpetrator with the strap of her shoulder bag and tightening it around her neck until she dropped the dolls.

A Kansas City postman flew to London to get a doll for his five-year-old when he heard the British had not yet come down with Cabbage Patch Fever.

One of the funniest stories found in every paper came from Milwaukee, where a disk jockey had announced in jest that a B-29 bomber would fly over the County Stadium with 2000 dolls available for those who would show up with a catcher's mitt and a credit card, to be photographed from the plane. Ridiculous though this caper might sound, desperate people deprived of their senses showed up and were furious at the announcer when no air drop took place.

Newsweek, in their article entitled, "What a doll! The Cabbage Patch Craze," wrote:

> It was as if an army had been turned loose on the nation's shopping malls, ravaging the *Ficus* trees, sloshing through the fountains, searching for the legendary stockrooms said to be filled with thousands of dough-faced, chinless, engagingly homely dolls that have become the Holy Grail of the 1983 Christmas shopping season: the Cabbage Patch Kids.[2]

Not only did the papers and TV tell the lurid tales of the search for "The Holy Grail," but important people felt led to make profound statements on the phenomenon.

Dr. Joyce Brothers "endorsed the dolls as healthy playthings for children."[3]

The Boston Children's Museum performed a mass adoption ceremony for the media.

Jane Pauley interviewed a group of Kids on the *Today Show*.

The Americans for Democratic Action "put the doll on its annual list of the Ten Best Toys, citing the doll's very ugliness as a significant point in its favor. It inculcates the important value of a non-discrimination on the basis of appearance."[4]

The National Institute of Infant Services announced that they are making natural cotton diapers available for the dolls.

> Special Cabbage Patch-size diapers are being offered by the cloth diaper services and can be purchased at cost or rented from some 200 metropolitan diaper services across the country. The Cabbage Patch baby is the big story this Christmas and we want to provide the happy ending.[5]

Bob Orben summed up his feelings as he wrote:

> They say a Cabbage Patch Kid is just like your own children—They are expensive, have a vacant expression, and are never around when you want one.[6]

If the old saying, "Imitation is the sincerest form of flattery," is true, the Cabbage Patch Kids should surely be flattered.

A Los Angeles cooking teacher Ruth Greenwold has created "The Real Cabbage Patch Doll." Its head is a real cabbage with eyes of tiny leaves held on by whole cloves for the pupils. The body is a flat-bottom squash with a corn husk cape and a hat of geranium leaves.

Two Baylor University students in Waco, Texas, came up with an answer to the shortage of Cabbage Patch Kids by creating the next best thing: a Cole-slaw Doll. Each one is an original with stuffed heads attached to Kerr canning jars that contain shredded fabric to look like coleslaw. Scott Huie and Dave Risinger, both chemistry majors, made the first dolls as a spoof, but at $8.99 apiece they sold so well that the young men kept manufacturing dolls and making money. Huie said:

> You tell someone, "I couldn't find you a Cabbage Patch Doll and so I got you this instead."

With the glass body it's difficult to cuddle, so Risinger stated, "It's even more useless than a Cabbage Patch Doll."[7]

Gene Buck, a public relations man from Pacific Grove, California, has come up with a Garbage Patch Doll—one that smells bad, looks worse, and will probably throw up in your car. In a tongue-in-cheek interview he said:

> What we're doing is to try and relate our dolls to kids because most kids are really ugly. Most dolls sit in a corner for weeks, but kids use our dolls right away because they start out dirty to begin with.

As an added bonus, each Garbage Patch Doll comes with its own felony arrest warrant.

When I was working on this book in the beauty parlor, Steve Hairdresser, as we call him, asked what the subject was. When I said, "Cabbage Patch Kids," he was excited! "My daughter Ashley has two of those dolls and a new Preemie." He then had to explain to me that Preemies are the new Cabbage Patch Kids who are born "prematurely."

Within one year the Cabbage Patch Kid has become an American institution and a model for imitation. Where will this instant legend go from here?

FUTURE APPRECIATION

My son-in-law Randall Briggs operates the Stamp and Coin Galleries in San Bernardino, California. He deals in a variety of collectibles, anything that within reason will appreciate in value: stamps, coins, silver, gold, coronation items, Wedgwood, relics, and limited editions. During the weeks before Christmas 1983, Cabbage Patch Kids suddenly appeared listed on his teletype machine as collectibles. They sold ten dolls from between $80 and $100 apiece!

We could hardly believe that people would pay these amounts for *new* dolls selling, if available, for $20 in the stores. Soon we heard of people who bought a Cabbage Patch Kid in a toy store and were mobbed in the parking lot by distraught parents who pleaded to buy the dolls for $50 to $150. Some made instant profits and some hung tight and fought their way to the car.

Blacks who had bought white dolls and whites who had bought black dolls met on corners and swapped.

As Coleco saw that they had a potential Shirley

Temple triumph on their hands, they came up with an added feature to insure the collectibility of their product. All dolls manufactured in 1983 had a black "birthmark" on their rears, so they simply changed the color of the ink to green for 1984 and produced an instant limited edition collector's item.

Yesterday I sat in a restaurant next to a couple with a little girl. She had a Cabbage Patch Doll on each side of her, and I asked about how long she had had them. Immediately she pulled down the back of the diaper and said, "See this black mark? That means she was born in 1983, but this other one has a green signature, showing she was made in 1984. I'm going to get a new one every year."

In celebration of his five years in the business, Xavier Roberts created two Champagne Anniversary Models signed on the rear end by Roberts himself. They were named Andre and Madeira and their adoption papers cost $1000, although it is assumed that they are worth over $2000 by now.

Lord and Taylor, a New York-based department store, is advertising "Our newest Cabbage Patch Kids—now on cozy, lovable slippers. Children will delight in adorable little faces looking up from giant plush slippers." These new additions to the Patch come in pink-and-lilac for girls and blue for boys. They are guaranteed to be genuine, from the Original Appalachian Artwork, and they cost only $17 a pair.

On Sunday, July 22, 1984, 300 people gathered in Yucaipa, California, for the First Annual Cabbage Patch Kid Fashion Show. The judges studied the homemade clothes on each doll. Paula Terri was in white organdy with silver slippers. Andre Pierre lounged in a Hawaiian flower print shirt. Phyllis Sally looked chubby in a black vinyl Playboy Bunny outfit, but she came out the winner.

Marilyn Meyer, participant from Rialto, said:

> It's sort of like a fever. You get one of these
> kids and can't resist getting more. When
> I bought my first one my friends thought
> I was crazy. Then they saw the values go
> up.[8]

A New England day camp for girls had a Cabbage Patch Day when each child was to bring her own doll to show off. One mother was complaining to a friend of mine that it wasn't fair to have this kind of discriminating program, since her daughter didn't have a Cabbage Patch Doll. My friend suggested that she might borrow one just for the day, but the lady looked horrified as she replied, "It would be easier to borrow someone's Mercedes than a Cabbage Patch Doll!"

When an item is scarce, when it's compared to a Mercedes, and when its values go up quickly, everyone has to have one. Why did this pudgy, homely doll become an overnight success?

2

Why Are the Cabbage Patch Kids So Popular?

When our daughters Lauren and Marita were children, they played with Barbie Dolls, perfect dolls manufactured with precision. When you bought a Barbie you knew she would be just like the last one: tall, slim, blonde, and elegant. You never had to worry that you might grab a Barbie box and get home to find that she had flabby thighs or jiggly arms. She never had dull eyes or blotchy skin, and her hair was never limp, lank, or lifeless.

Barbie lived a fairy-tale existence in her Barbie house, her Barbie car, and her Barbie yacht. Her biggest decision in life was which of 500 outfits to choose from her Barbie closet. Would she opt for tennis, climb the Matterhorn, or play water polo? To make her pursuits complete, Barbie married Ken, who also lived the life of the idle rich and didn't come with work clothes that a person would need to paint a garage or change light bulbs.

Barbie and Ken, assembly-line productions, predicted for their small hosts a perfect future with perfect bodies—a future where long-legged bodies lounged by pools and got up once an hour to change clothes, a future where all husbands came with portfolios full of inheritance and had nothing more pressing on their minds than which tuxedo to wear to the opera.

The Barbie-Ken existence represents what we had all hoped for in the '50s and '60s: If we work hard enough we'll get to Utopia and live happily ever after. So we did the right things, joined the right clubs, and moved into identical tract homes. Later we got refrigerators with ice cubes leaping out of the door toward the microwave oven. We had hardly warmed up to our hot tubs when we were told being a Barbie Doll wasn't real. All housewives became dull and boring. We were to get out and find ourselves. We suddenly needed fulfillment for our feelings. Children became a drag, and if you must have a few, at least put them in daycare. The single life brought bliss. Extricate yourself from dependencies and involvements. Develop meaningful and undemanding relationships. If it feels good, do it!

All this confusion, this deviation from what we grew up expecting, has produced lonely children, single, working-parent homes, latchkey kids, and stepfamilies.

"Ever after" has come, and it's not happy. Isolated children and introspective parents have packed Barbie and Ken into a steamer trunk and sent them off to the Riviera for a long-awaited vacation.

Onto the stage to fill the void has come a nursery

full of little Cabbage Patch Kids who are, in contrast to Barbie and Ken:

Unique: Guaranteed to be one-of-a-kind.

In need: Arms outstretched in search of a mother.

Adoptable: Wanting to really belong to someone.

UNIQUE

We've come full circle. We wanted factories with production control that could turn out identical goods, and we got them. We've done so well that from the rear we all seem to be named Levi, Gloria Vanderbilt, Ralph Lauren, Gucci, Bill Blass, or Calvin Klein.

So what do we long for? Something different. Something uniquely ours. Something not uniformly perfect. A Cabbage Patch Doll of Life.

Coleco did more than manufacture a new toy—they caught the deep desires in human nature to want something that no one else has.

The *New York Times* News Service wrote:

> The Cabbage Patch Kids—those pudgy, homely, soft little dolls with no chins that seemed to be just about everywhere during the holidays—were so extraordinarily popular because they were designed to be substitute children, according to researchers and psychologists who helped with the development of the dolls."[9]

"Substitute children." In this era when women have been told that having children is old-fashioned, it is fascinating to see that even those who follow this trend still have maternal instincts. They don't have the time for a child who needs to be fed, but the researchers for Cabbage Patch found that these women would buy dolls to mother.

A 35-year-old checker at the supermarket asked a friend of mine who had a new baby if she would give her some of the clothes when she was done with them. "Do you have a new baby too?" my friend asked.

"No, I just have a Cabbage Patch Doll. She fills my need for children."

During our Maine vacation I found one little girl who takes her Cabbage Patch Doll's temperature every day to see if she's sick. I also spotted a little four-year-old boy with an adorable but very soiled Cabbage Patch Kid. I asked him the doll's name and he told me it was Alan Ezra.

I said to his mother, "He must have had Alan a long time."

"Oh, no," she replied. "Only three months. It looks worn out because he hasn't let it out of his hands since we got it."

She then explained to me that three months ago she had lost a baby in childbirth, and to make up to the little boy for the brother that never came home from the hospital, she had bought him the doll as a substitute baby.

As she shared this touching story with me, the child clutched little Alan to his chest as if afraid someone might take him away. This transfer of affection has been so effective that I wonder what will happen to the boy emotionally if he ever loses his substitute brother. Will it become a second death instead of the misplacing of a toy?

Coleco has created "substitute children" for those who for one reason or another can't have the real thing. They have capitalized on the human need to possess something uniquely ours.

The News Service article continues:

> The Cabbage Patch Dolls were not beauti-
> ful, and we know that babies are not
> always beautiful. Equally important was
> the *concept of uniqueness*. Using com-
> puters to keep track of its dolls, the com-
> pany despite having almost three million
> of the dolls produced in Hong Kong, says
> it has managed to keep each one individual
> by changing characteristics such as eye
> color, freckles, hair, dimples and clothing.
> Each doll is different, so it became true
> that nobody has a doll like yours.[10]

The "concept of uniqueness" is the genius stroke
made by the manufacturers of these little tykes. Each
one has its own look and its own name. All Barbies
were Barbies and Kens were Kens, and who would
rename Chatty Cathy? When I as a child had a
Shirley Temple Doll, would I have called her Agnes?
Dolls have all been duplicates of each other, but not
the Cabbage Patch Kids. Each doll has its own name
written on the birth certificate, guaranteeing both
its uniqueness and its place as a substitute child.

Dale Carnegie has promoted the idea that the
sweetest sound to any person is the sound of his own
name. My husband, Fred, in his genuine concern for
others, listens intently to each person's name and
makes a point of remembering it. Within two days
at the lodge during our vacation, Fred knew 40 people and was calling them by name as they entered
for meals or passed by the shuffleboard court. Not
one person failed to brighten up and smile as Fred
showed he cared enough to learn who they were.
People would come over to Fred when they wanted

to know someone's name, and he became the hub of camp information.

Everybody wants to be somebody, and a good name is what we each desire. In Proverbs it says:

> A good name is rather to be chosen than great riches, and loving favor rather than silver and gold.[11]

Ecclesiastes adds:

> A good name is better than precious ointment.[12]

In the early church men with names "of good report" were chosen to run the business of the church;[13] Cornelius was said to have a good name among all the nations.[14] Timothy was well-reported of by the brethren.[15] Ananias had a good name with all who dwelt in Damascus,[16] and Demetrius was of good report of all who knew him.[17]

We all want a good name, and we have a natural pride in our reputation. We want our names to be spelled correctly and pronounced well. We want to know where our name came from and what it means. I'm glad I am "flourishing and blooming" and that Fred is a "peaceful ruler." I checked recently and found a bookstore that has three different volumes on the meaning of names. When I was on "100 Huntley Street" TV in Toronto, David Mainse gave me one book from a series of five on the names of Jesus Christ by Charles Rolls. In 215 pages Dr. Rolls covers only those names of Jesus which begin with the letters A to G: Alpha, Author of Salvation, Almighty, Advocate, Anchor, All in All, Gift, Guide, Governor,

Gatherer, etc. For us believers the Bible promises:

> I will give them an everlasting name that
> shall not be cut off.[18]

We have such a fascination with names that by giving each Cabbage Patch Kid a unique name, the makers benefit from our curiosity. One lady told me her little girl with her Cabbage Patch Doll was stopped everywhere she went by adults who would ask, "What's her name?"—the doll, not the child! This would open up a pleasant conversation with the girl and her doll as the center of attention. The little brother asked for a doll, but his mother pointed out that boys don't play with dolls. He answered quickly, "I don't want to play with it, I just want to carry it so people will talk to me."

Cabbage Patch Dolls are attention-getters. Each one is individually made, is a substitute child, and has its own name on the birth certificate. Each Cabbage Patch Kid is guaranteed to be *unique.*

IN NEED

While Barbie and Ken start life as adults and are obviously self-sufficient, the little babes found in the Cabbage Patch need help. Each one looks so pathetic once you see it in a store that you can't leave it on a shelf to fend for itself. You know it can't face the hard, cruel world alone.

Do you remember the fleeting Christmas some 20 years ago when a toy company, way ahead of the times, produced Pitiful Pearl? Poor Pitiful was all that Lauren wanted that year, and I could hardly bring myself to pay money for something that looked as if it belonged in the trash. Pitiful Pearl wore ugly cotton stockings and black oxfords. Her dress and tattered apron were patched. Her face reflected perpetual depression, and her long blonde hair was straight and stringy. Tying this pathetic look together was a red babushka on her head, giving her the look of just getting out of a concentration camp.

Lauren loved her and mended her, but poor Pitiful never caught on, and her brief unshining hour soon burned out.

What a hit she could be today, nestled sadly in the Cabbage Patch waiting patiently for someone to want her!

Psychologists have told us for years that our greatest human desire, after self-preservation, is to be needed. We desperately want someone who needs us. We can be told convincingly that we will be happier alone, but underneath we want someone who cares.

> It is not good for the man to be alone. I will make a helper suitable for him.[19]

Dr. Lee Salk, professor of pediatrics and psychology at Cornell University Medical College, suggests that the Cabbage Patch Kids brought out the possessiveness in people and "underscored children's identity with parents, their need for a sense of belonging."[20]

Dr. Paul Horton, author of *Solace*, a study of humans' need for objects to care for, says that children "need attachments external to themselves to give solace and comfort. A Cabbage Patch Kid is a possession a child is instantly able to make his own."[21]

Ruth Manko, a psychologist and market researcher

who studied parents' and children's reactions to the Kids, said:

> They responded to the outstretched arms, read the birth certificates and adoption papers. We showed them the belly-buttons. They all wore Pampers, and the mothers related to them right away.[22]

The Cabbage Patch Kid appeals not only to children but to mothers who see their children growing up and not needing them anymore. The maternal instinct, the desire to care for something helpless, is so strong in us women that even if our rational minds tell us we don't want children, we still respond to the outstretched arms of a baby. We all want something that can't get along without us.

Child psychologist Doris McNeely Johnson calls it "a universal need that children have to hold something and cuddle it."[23]

Brandeis University psychologist Malcolm Watson points out that the Cabbage Patch Kids—

> . . .constitute a releasing mechanism that triggers the instinct for nurturing in both adults and children. The same powerful instinct that makes you want to pick up and hug a baby in his crib has been harnessed to make you want to snatch a $25 toy off the shelf.[24]

The Cabbage Patch Kids are not adorable dream babies, they're not Kewpie Dolls, but as the *Newsweek* writers said so well:

> Their ugliness has a touching runt-of-the-

litter quality that adults and children alike find irresistible. . . . Without actually resembling any real baby that has ever walked the earth—for which the whole human race can be grateful—Cabbage Patch Kids caricature almost every characteristic of babyness: blunt, fat features; round cheeks; big eyes; short, pudgy little arms and legs.[25]

Most of us know some intelligent woman who continues to date what we consider a bum, but when questioned says, "But he needs me." Most of us know some businessman who's left a competent wife for an insipid clinging vine because "she needs me."

There will always be people in need who will touch our hearts in one way or another.

Jesus said, "The poor you will always have with you."[26]

Welfare aid and psychiatrists will not eliminate those who are poor of possessions or poor in spirit.

For the poor shall never cease out of the land; therefore I command thee, saying, Thou shalt open thine hand wide unto thy brother, to thy poor and to the needy in thy land.[27]

Defend the poor and fatherless; do justice to the afflicted and the needy.[28]

God gave us the desire to care for those in need, and taught us, "It is more blessed to give than to receive."[29]

ADOPTABLE

The Cabbage Patch Kids are surely unique, and

their helpless look has brought out the protective spirit in millions of children and adults who need to be needed. If that combination isn't enough, these babies are adoptable. We don't just buy them as we do bicycles—we adopt them.

Children who have every new toy that TV promotes soon tire of the latest thing and have no lasting attachment to the passing parade of puzzles and panda bears. But the Cabbage Patch Kids demand a relationship. They make their owner grow up and become responsible. They present the new parent with a document. They ask not only for a place to sit, but a place in the parent's heart. They want a signature on the dotted line. They cry for commitment. They're available for adoption. What a powerful combination!

The dictionary defines "adopt" as taking voluntarily as one's own what is not so naturally. Surely no one has given birth to a Cabbage Patch Kid, but millions of people have voluntarily adopted them. Adoption also implies that you've signed, that your ownership is secure. No one can take this child away from you. He becomes part of your family. He belongs.

Children take these dolls everywhere; they even get high chairs for them in restaurants. While Fred and I were vacationing, eight-year-old-Laurie brought her Cabbage Patch Kid to the table. I asked the doll's name and she replied, "Jolean Leann Ladley."

"Did she come with three names?"

"No, Ladley is my last name. I put it on her because that's what you do when you adopt a baby—you give her your name."

"Of course," I replied to her simple wisdom.

Her mother then added, "It wasn't easy to get this

doll. We were on a waiting list from last January until July."

"But it was worth the wait."

Laurie smiled as she clutched Jolean to her blouse.

"What do you like best about her?" I asked.

She thought a few seconds and answered, "Just that she's mine."

Isn't that what we want—something that's really ours! It may not be beautiful or useful, but "It's mine."

Adopting a baby versus buying a doll causes a child to become responsible in an irresponsible world; it offers security during insecure situations.

It's amazing how the Cabbage Patch Dolls appeal to our inner desires to have something uniquely our own, to possess someone who really needs us, and to adopt a being whose call for commitment brings out responsible behavior.

3

How Can Barbie and Ken Live Happily Ever After?

Yes, we are a nation of Cabbage Patch Kids who are unique, in need, and adoptable; but there are many other kinds of human dolls who feel they've come off an assembly line, have little worthwhile identity, seem to be shoved on a shelf, and don't think anyone is going to buy them, take them home, and include them as part of the family.

I meet many Barbie Dolls. They've exercised, eaten their fiber, and bought new clothes. They've taken courses to find themselves or followed gurus to grope for truth. But they still don't know who they are, no one seems to need them or sense their needs, and even though surrounded by people, they're lonely and don't seem to belong.

They've often married, or recently divorced, Ken Dolls who have given them homes, cars, and maybe

even yachts, but who have never given of themselves because they're not sure who they are and
do better with distant and undemanding relationships.

Many of the dolls I meet are Cheerful Tearfuls,
laughing on the outside but crying on the inside,
trying to pretend that their life is in order by hiding
how hurt and lonesome they really are.

In every group there is a scattering of Pitiful
Pearls, those who have given up, those who know
there is no hope for them. They may not have tattered clothes, but they have patches on their hearts.

I have such compassion when I meet these people because I've been on their shelf myself. Because
I had few possessions as a child, I aimed for a Barbie Doll existence. I married a Ken named Fred and
planned to live happily ever after. My first two little dolls were beautiful and perfect and even had
their own playhouse on the back lawn. We lived
what appeared to be a fairy-tale existence.

My third child broke the bubble. When I learned
from the doctor that Freddie was hopelessly brain-
damaged, I went from Cheerful to Tearful. I pre-
tended to be brave on the outside, but I was crying
on the inside. I was angry at God that He would let
a terrible trauma like this happen to Fred and me.

We did the best we could in these trying circumstances, and we kept ourselves occupied so we
wouldn't have to deal with how we really felt.
While I was in the hospital having our fourth baby,
Lawrence Chapman Littauer, Fred put his namesake
in a private hospital and we tried in vain to pretend
we had never had him.

When Larry was six months old, little Freddie
died, and Fred and I were forced to face the reality
of the death of our son. We didn't talk about it to

anyone, and through our hidden tears we tried to be brave.

One week after Freddie died, I found out that my little Larry had the same brain damage. I didn't think I could live through such agony again. We took him to a brain specialist, and I sat before this doctor like a Pitiful Pearl begging him to give me some hope. I was crying on the inside and on the outside as he looked up and said, "You've been through this before—you know there is no hope."

Where do you turn when you know there is no hope?

I had no answers; my church seemed to ignore my problems. But I had a sister-in-law who had been praying for me, and one day she took me to a Christian women's club. The speaker pointed at me as he said, "There may be someone here today who looks good on the outside, but she knows she's miserable inside."

"How does he know me?" I thought. "I must be the only one here with problems, and it must show."

He mentioned that we all have problems, but that our own always seem the worst because they are unique to us. But when we recognize our *need*, and know we can't handle life alone, the Lord Jesus is ready to come into our broken hearts and give us joy even in adverse circumstances.

Even though I knew the Lord had never had a case just like mine before, I was so desperate for some hope that I was willing to give this man's play a try.

*Present your bodies a living sacrifice.
    Why not? I wasn't worth much anyway!

*Be not conformed to the world.
    I had already tried that routine.

  *Be transformed by the renewing of your
  mind.
      I sure needed a new mind!
  *Know the good, acceptable, and perfect will
  of God.
      I don't think God has a good will toward
      me, but I'll take the chance.

I prayed quietly in my heart following the words
the speaker gave. Then he concluded, "You're now
part of the family of God. Find a good church and
follow what God has in mind for you."

Within weeks Fred and I were both back in
church and studying God's Word. What had been
dull before took on new meaning as we committed
our lives to the Lord and searched for hope in our
time of need.

We learned that we were *unique*.

"The Lord thy God has chosen thee to be a special people unto himself...because [He] loved
you."[30]

We realized that God knew of our *needs*, even as
he knew of David's:

      Have mercy on me, O Lord, for I am
      weak.... I am weary with my groaning;
      all night I make my bed to swim; I water
      my couch with my tears. Mine eye is con-
      sumed because of grief...the Lord hath
      heard the voice of my weeping. The Lord
      hath heard my supplication; the Lord will
      receive my prayer.[31]

We found, as we expressed our needs and called
to Him, that He made us part of His family forever:

As many as received him, to them gave
he the power to become the sons of God.[32]

God *adopts* us:

By the Spirit's power we cry out to God,
"Father! My Father!" God's Spirit...de-
clares that we are God's children.[33]

Now we know we are not alone, "not foreigners
or strangers any longer, [but] fellow-citizens with
God's people and members of the family of God."[34]

So many people today are like Fred and me, good
people who mean well but who have so many problems of life holding them down that their unique
needs leave them empty and alone. How about you?
Do you long for some everlasting arms to enfold you,
to pick you up, to cuddle you, to *adopt* you into the
family?

If you're still sitting out in the Cabbage Patch, not
sure you're any different from those in the next row,
waiting for someone to sense you're special and to
pick you up...

If you have many burdens but have been disap-
pointed because people haven't met your needs...

If you're lonesome, even in crowds, and want to
belong to an eternal family and feel secure...

Then make this prayer your own and claim these
Scriptures for your new life.

Dear Lord Jesus,
I've never felt I was *unique*, but the Bible
tells me that You are God's only begotten
Son[35] and that You are truly unique. The
Word also tells me that when I realize my

need and ask You to come into my life and change me, then I "have the mind of Christ" and "become a new creature"[36] and "put on the new man."[37] I am "called by a new name"[38] and am unique, chosen, special.

I ask You, Lord Jesus, to take me, a *unique* person, *in need* and *adoptable*, into the family of God. Thank You for promising that I will never be alone again, for You said, "Lo, I am with you always, even unto the end of the world."[39]

Amen

In legal human adoption we sign papers that guarantee this child is ours and assure him he is secure in our family. As you have committed your life to the Lord, you have become secure in God's family.

You heard the true message, the Good News that brought you salvation. You believed in Christ, and God put his stamp of ownership on you by giving you the Holy Spirit he had promised. The Spirit is the guarantee that we shall receive what God has promised his people.[40]

Yes, you are now secure in God's family! He has put His stamp of ownership upon you, and you will receive your inheritance as He has promised.

God so loved you—a unique, special person—that He sent His only begotten Son that if you—in your need—would believe in Him, He would take you into the family, would not allow you to perish, and would give you everlasting life.[41]

God wants to adopt us all, and He has given us personal examples in the Old Testament. When Jacob was close to death he adopted his two grandsons by Joseph—Ephraim and Manasseh—so they could receive an inheritance. He said, "They are mine.... Let my name be named on them."[42]

Moses was adopted. His birth mother "brought him unto Pharaoh's daughter, and he became her son. And she called his name Moses. And she said, Because I drew him out of the water."[43]

Queen Esther was adopted. "And he [Mordecai] brought up Esther, his uncle's daughter; for she had neither father nor mother, and the maid was fair and beautiful, whom Mordecai, when her father and mother were dead, took for his own daughter."[44]

God wants each one of us in His family. He wants to say, "They are mine. Let my name be named on them."[45]

He wants to draw us out of our troubled waters and make us His own.

He sees us as fair and beautiful, as *unique* individuals, *in need* of a Savior, available for *adoption*.

4

Is Life Any Deeper Than Silly Putty?

What value is there in spending these moments reflecting on the current fad of the Cabbage Patch Kids? Is there something to be learned here a little deeper than Slinky and Silly Putty? Have the manufacturers produced something more than a successful toy?

The answer is yes if we care to apply this lesson to our own lives and to our relationships with our families.

UNIQUE

We all want to feel that we are special. In my closing message in my Christian Leaders And Speakers Seminar (C.L.A.S.S.), I share our desire to be special. I quote Paul telling Timothy that he is his chosen man—he's special, he's unique.

I tell of my relationship with my grandson Randy. Because both of my sons were born with irreversible brain damage, we had concern over our daughter Lauren's first pregnancy. My Bible study ladies and I prayed over 2 Timothy 1:7:

> For God has not given us the spirit of fear,
> but of power, and of love, and of a sound
> mind.

We claimed that this baby would be a special boy with a sound mind, and he is. When he was four his testing showed that he had the vocabulary of an eight-year-old. I've never cared if he were athletic or musical, only that he have a "sound mind."

Right from the beginning I let him know he was special to me, that I prayed for him long before he was born. One day I told him that my two baby boys had died. He asked, "Didn't you take them to the doctor? Wouldn't they take their medicine?" I tried to explain that this problem was one that no one could solve, but because of losing my boys he was very special to me.

"You are my special boy," I reported.

When I leave on a speaking trip I explain, "Randy, Grammie's going to tell the ladies that you are her special boy."

When I return he asks, "Did you tell the ladies I'm special?"

"I surely did Randy, and they'd all love to meet you."

One day I went to pick him up at nursery school, and the teacher asked him if he'd like to introduce his grandmother. He took me by the hand, led me over to where the children were sitting in a circle on the floor, and said, "This is my grammie and I am her special boy."

Every time I tell this story I get a lump in my throat and sometimes tears in my eyes as I share that I have a boy who knows he's special. The audience listens reflectively and often tearfully as I ask, "Do you have a special boy? Do you make someone know he's special?"

Although we can't make other people choose us as special, we have the power to give others the unique feeling of being special. What a gift we bestow—far better than a new doll—when we pin the label SPECIAL on a child, on a note, on a friend, on a lonely elder.

We all want to be that chosen person; we want to be loved. So many sad and lonely people I talk to are waiting for someone to find them, to make them special; yet the best way to find this unique relationship is to give it away to someone else.

As I continue to tell Randy he's my special boy, I become a special person to him. If he has a choice of whom to sit with, why would he select a person he's not sure of when he knows he's secure with me?

Everyone wants to be considered *unique*. We don't want to be just run-of-the-mill. So let someone know he's special today, and you'll become special tomorrow.

IN NEED

Are there people *in need* in our affluent society? We all think of those ads showing starving children in Africa. My mother goaded me into eating everything on my plate by bemoaning the plight of the starving children in China. Not many of us know any of these deprived individuals personally, and a contribution to charity here or there eases our conscience, but we overlook the emotional needs of our own family and friends because they look well-fed. They may even be overweight. They may have designer clothes, a decorated living room, and a pedigreed dog, but these are often cover-ups for the problems underneath.

What we need more than anything else is someone who cares enough to listen to our needs. We don't think anyone really understands us—and they don't. They haven't had time to listen; as one man told me, "I'd rather pretend everything's all right than have to face the problems."

Why does a businessman pour his whole life out to some young thing he met at the water cooler? Because he doesn't think his wife really cares—and she may not. He's not attracted to this girl for her beauty or brains, but because she sensed he had a need to share his needs, and she was available to listen. I've had wives ask me, "What can he see in her? She's plain and simpleminded and hasn't got half my talent. What has she got that I don't have?"

It isn't *what she's got*, it's *how she makes him feel*. She seems to understand his needs.

Why do many women go crying to the pastor? Because their husband won't listen to their problems. He tells them to "keep quiet" or "forget it," and they can't do either.

Some throw themselves emotionally, and some physically, upon their pastor, who sometimes isn't too satisfied with his own marital situation. His wife is sick of him giving his life for the needs of others, and she's turned cold. He knows she has a valid point, but he doesn't think she really understands what *he* goes through.

So there he sits, spiritual and unsatisfied, while some sad lady sobs on his shirt.

How easy it is to back up and look at these current scenes and see how unfulfilled needs can lead to trouble!

In C.L.A.S.S. I have a lesson titled "We've Got Troubles Right Here In River City." Initially this was to show the needs of our community that we as Christian leaders should be able to fill. I had altruistic ideals that those of us who have it all together should minister to those who don't. What an optimistic thought!

For my very first C.L.A.S.S. I personally invited the participants: exceptional women who were already leaders, speakers, and / or teachers. I knew their abilities and felt I knew their personal lives. The weekend before C.L.A.S.S. started I spoke at a retreat. An elegant lady named Nancy came out of the audience to tell me that God had told her she was to come to C.L.A.S.S. I explained that I had chosen these women because I knew them, but I surely did not wish to second-guess God. She flew home with me on the plane and told me that when she was 11 years old she had been raped in church on the organ bench by the head elder. I was aghast and told her she would be the only one in the group with such a story.

On the second evening it was her turn to share, and she told how she practiced the organ every Saturday afternoon in church, then how the elder grabbed her from behind and raped her on the organ bench. Nancy's message left everyone drained but grateful that the Lord had led her to proper counsel and ultimately a victory which had prepared her to help others in similar need.

When Nancy was through, Lauren whispered in

my ear, "There are two ladies crying in the rest-room." I went in to find two sisters sobbing, and when they were able to talk one shared that when they were children their father had committed incest with her while her sister lay terrified in the same bed. They had never shared one word of this between them, but Nancy's story had caused them to open up and let loose pent-up emotions that they had kept under wraps for years.

As they had a time to lift their burdens together, Lauren came to tell me two ladies were crying in the hall. She led me to them, and I learned that one had been raped in church as a teenager but had never told anyone, and the other had a sister who was in deep regressive therapy at that moment as the result of a gang rape which had occurred when she was only eight.

While they were sharing with each other I went to find Nancy, who was counseling a lady whose father had molested her and her girlfriends she had brought home from college. Standing waiting was another lady whose 14-year-old-daughter had locked herself in her room because she had been raped on the way home from school.

I was overwhelmed, dumbfounded, and confused, but Nancy wasn't, for within a few minutes she had these six together in the ladies' lounge, where she shared, counseled, and prayed with them. Although she could not erase their past experiences, she understood their needs and she could give them hope that those of us without similar problems could never give.

From that moment on, I realized that there are troubles right here in River City, and that each one of us can deal with the needs of others according to our own experiences. I can feel the heartache of a woman who has lost a child or has one who is retarded. Nancy can commiserate with and give hope to a rape victim. We don't have to do research to study areas of need; we only need to open our eyes and be available, and the Lord will show us those whom we can help.

In our small group sessions in C.L.A.S.S., each participant is asked to introduce himself or herself. We don't ask them to bare their souls, and yet within a matter of minutes people are sharing their needs openly in front of a group of people they don't even know. Why? Because so many have been stuffing their concerns down inside them, assuming that no one else has any problems or that the Christian community would judge them as less than spiritual if they opened their mouths. Given an opportunity to honestly state how they feel, the words pour out like a waterfall.

During our staff meeting at night we aim to pair people-with-problems with people-with-answers so that the following day we can get them together and personally meet their needs.

At our last C.L.A.S.S. I passed out a "Trouble In River City" chart and asked each person to check off from the 50 problems any with which they had had personal experience. They were not to indicate their names because we wanted them to be honest. When we tallied them up, out of 80 women and a few men we had:

15 Who were alcoholics or were married to one.
10 Involved in drugs in some way.
14 Victims of rape or incest.
 4 Eating disorders.
 2 Attempted suicide.

5 Involved with victims of violent
crimes.
3 Who had been abandoned children.
2 Abused children.
7 Lost children to death.
7 Terminal illnesses.
10 Single parents.

As I read the totals in our closing session of "The
Troubles Right Here In River City," it was easy to
see that we didn't have to leave that room to find
people in need.

The Christian community is full of people in need,
people standing with buckets of burdens waiting
for others with armloads of answers. We don't have
to be perfect to help those in need; we only have
to be willing to share what we've learned through
our own experiences in order that we might give
others hope.

For God did not comfort us that we might be com-
fortable but that we might comfort others.

"Comfort ye my people, saith your God."[46]

ADOPTABLE

Xavier Roberts knew when he created his $125
doll with adoption papers that human nature doesn't
place much value on that which costs little, or stay
connected with that which has demanded no
commitment.

For the last 15 years we have been in what Thomas
Wolfe labeled "The ME Generation." We have been
told to look out for number one. Young people have
been asked to avoid commitments of any type
because commitments breed responsibility and

responsibility chokes out freedom. This philosophy of life has produced flocks of immature adults who are in headlong pursuits of personal pleasure and who flee relationships that get within sight of responsibility. This hedonistic heaven was going to free us all up and remove our repressions in a reward of riotous living, but there are more people with emotional problems now than ever before.

What is there left to do? How much further can we go? We can hope that *Time* magazine is correct when it states on its cover, "Sex In The 80's—The Revolution Is Over."[47] The article tells us that we've gone about as far as we can go, and I was encouraged to learn that "there is growing evidence that the national obsession with sex is subsiding."[48]

There may be some of you who didn't even know there was a sexual revolution, and a few of you who are disturbed that the whole thing's over before you ever joined up.

One San Francisco sex therapist said:

> We've been going through a ME generation; now I see people wanting to get back into the WE generation.[49]

Another states:

> Total growth, total narcissism, which is supposed to fix everything, doesn't.[50]

A Chicago graduate student wrote:

> What women who tried to break out of traditional relationships found is that it doesn't work.[51]

Summing up the essence of the article, one could say that free love has not solved problems and that the emotional health of those opting for relationships

without responsibility is shaky at best. The conclu-
sion is that we don't value that which we aren't committed to.

In the Bible Paul says to Timothy about his faith
in God:

> I know whom I have believed, and am
> persuaded that he is able to keep that
> which I have *committed* unto him against
> that day.[52]

Paul knows that God will watch over that part of
his life which he has *committed*. We as humans are
the same: We make an effort to watch over, keep
an eye on, that which has been *committed* into our
responsibility. In this one secular cover article the
word *commitment*, a word that has been out of
popular usage for years, was mentioned many times.

> The buzz words these days are "commit-
> ment," "intimacy," and working at
> relationships.
>
> Expressing longings for vanished intimacy
> and the now-elusive joys of romance and
> *commitment.*
>
> We are seeking a balance. We realize that
> revolving-door sex is not the answer to
> true love and *commitment*.
>
> Though many values are still being sorted
> out, most Americans seem stubbornly
> *committed* to family, marriage, and tradi-
> tional ideas.[53]

Isn't it encouraging that commitment is coming
back into style? Can we hope that it will be followed
by maturity and responsibility?

When a person adopts a baby or a mate, he takes

voluntarily as his own that which was not naturally his. We accept responsibility for the safekeeping of another person, and this gives us a feeling of worth. Commitment demands a price, but without it we have no value.

We are a nation of Cabbage Patch Kids. We want so much to be special, to be *unique*.

We are *in need* in so many different ways, and from our own experiences we are able to meet the needs of others.

We are *adoptable*, wanting a loving commitment from a mature and responsible person who will give us a measure of security.

Knowing these truths, what a blessing each one of us can be to other people when we make them feel special, listen to their needs (and help meet them), and commit ourselves to becoming responsible adults.

5

Is the Cabbage Patch Really in Boston?

When I share the message of this book with high school and college young people, I let them know that I have my very own Cabbage Patch Doll. Because they have grown up in the ME generation, where morals are a thing of the past and where the only measure is "If it feels good, do it," young people see no need for old-fashioned standards. Where parents divorce easily and where television pictures as the norm beautiful people hopping daily from bed to bed, young people see no need for commitment. Yet they crave attention in this lonely world. Their desire to be loved by someone often leads them into romantic involvements so readily available. They don't count the possible cost, and they assume, "It will never happen to me."

They can't imagine the lives that may be affected

by a fleeting fancy for someone of the opposite sex.

How did I adopt my Cabbage Patch Doll?

Over 20 years ago an adorable nurse in Connecticut took a chance. She had chestnut-brown curly hair and big brown eyes. She was a good girl who meant well and who was engaged to a handsome boy. A dashing Air Force lieutenant on a weekend pass swept her off her feet and left town, never to be heard from again. When she found she was pregnant, she moved out of the state so the people at home and at church wouldn't know what had happened. She spent lonely months in Boston waiting for the birth of her baby. On November 16, 1963, she had a little boy, and even though he looked just like her and she wanted to keep him, she gave him up for adoption, returned to Connecticut, and began life all over again, trying to forget the past.

At that same time Fred and I were struggling to get over the loss of our two sons. We had applied for adoption, and one day we received a call to say that a perfect baby boy was available. How excited Fred and I were as we drove those many miles to view this baby, who was then three months old! A nurse brought him out on a white eyelet pillow. His chestnut-brown curls framed his precious little face and his big brown eyes looked up to ask, "Who are you?"

It was love at first sight, and I wanted to take him home right then, but the caseworker said, "Think it over for a few days. We don't want you to make an emotional decision."

Lauren and Marita could hardly wait for a real baby, a brother who wouldn't be sick, who wouldn't be taken away from them.

Here was a baby who was *unique*, born of parents who should never have gotten together in the first place, born of an uncommitted young man and a young woman who never thought it would happen to her. He was a one-of-a-kind child, never to be duplicated again.

He was also *in need*. The foster mother who cared for him felt he was special, and she asked to keep him longer than usual, but even then she knew she couldn't raise him as her own. She named him Jeffrey and loved him dearly. We put Frederick in front of Jeffrey and loved him even more.

Most important to us was the fact that this *unique* baby, who *needed* a home, was *adoptable*; we could sign papers and be secure that he was ours alone. We opened our family heart to him. We chose him as our special boy. We adopted him: We took voluntarily as our own that which was not naturally ours.

From the beginning we told him that he was a special boy and that we chose him to be ours. He has always been an introspective and thoughtful child, and when he was ten he said to me, "Mother, I'm sorry for the problems you've had with your two boys, but I was just thinking that if it hadn't been for them I wouldn't be your son. I would have been born anyway, and someone else would have had me, but it wouldn't have been you, and I might not even be a Christian."

We are so grateful that God chose this beautiful boy, that he selected our sensitive son; and I'm so glad that the mythical Cabbage Patch really is in Boston and that it produced for us a child *unique*, *in need*, and *adoptable*.

6

What Will You Think Of?

From here on what will you think of when you see a Cabbage Patch Doll? What will pass through your mind as you view those little faces in the toy stores, in magazines, or in your own child's bed? How will you react when the special sale for the day is Cabbage Patch shoes for children or when you see a shelf of Cabbage Patch paper dolls with two different wigs to transform the little one from a girl to a boy?

Perhaps you'll remember the message in this book; perhaps you'll say to yourself, "They're popular because they're unique, in need, and adoptable." Then you'll apply these three thoughts to your own life.

If you have a low self-image, you can have God's assurance that He chose you to be His before the world was formed. He views you as unique, special, and one-of-a-kind. You can know that God sees you apart from the crowd; while you may feel insignificant, God knows the hairs on your head and has already appointed you to life forever with Him.

If you have a child who is nervous, who often misbehaves, who seems depressed, perhaps he's never felt secure or worthwhile. Possibly you or your mate have reprimanded him in ways that have broken his self-image. Perhaps he feels he's the dumb one, the clumsy one, or the bad one.

What can you do to change his self-opinion before it's too late? Will you start today to make him feel special? Will you take each child apart at least once a week and spend time listening to what's on his heart without rebuking him or telling him he's wrong? Will you stop comparing him with his brothers who are athletes, with his sisters who get better grades, with his friend who sits still? Will you find his strengths and review them with him? Will you let him know that there is a loving God who looks on him as special?

How about your partner? Do you make him feel that he is the most important person in life to you? So many men are in a period labeled "Midlife Crisis." They feel useless and worthless. They look around at a busy wife and children who ignore them, they sense their job is going nowhere, and they say, "Is this all there is to life?" We women can help prevent this devastation if we renew our goal of putting our husband first.

You men so often take your wives for granted. You don't realize how dull her life seems compared to the magazines touting the superwoman success. She gets no pay for laundry and dishes; she has no hope for advancement. Can you let her know you appreciate her efforts? Can you take the burden of the children off her at least once or twice a week? Can you uplift her, encourage her, and help her? Can you make her feel special?

We all want to be loved. We all want to receive praise and affection, but where is it going to come from if we don't begin to give it?

The next time you see a Cabbage Patch Kid, a unique creation, ask yourself what you've done lately to let someone else know he's really special.

When you watch a wistful child gazing longingly at her Cabbage Patch Doll, will you see those outstretched arms as a symbol of the needs we all have for someone who truly loves us, for someone who really cares? Will you remember that we all have needs, that we want someone who really understands us? When you see the longing look on the little doll, open and vulnerable, will you ask yourself if you've let your needs be known? Or are you sitting around waiting for someone to figure them out, playing a guessing game with the players of life?

So many of us sit on the shelf of self-pity, waiting for someone to recognize our needs and fill them. Why not open up to the members of your family or to a friend? So many say, "I could have helped if I had only known the problem."

How about looking around to find other people you can help? One of the best steps in overcoming depression is to take your eyes off your own problems and do something positive for someone else. Start with those closest to you, even though it is easier to send money to foreign missions. Ask each individual privately what needs he or she has that aren't being filled.

When we were raising our children and had family meetings we would ask what things they needed

done for them. One week it would be information
for a term paper and the next a light bulb in the
bathroom. We tried to meet the needs, whatever
they were. Even today Fred and I check with each
other frequently: "Is there anything you need that
I can fulfill?"

If you have been through a trauma in your life,
realize that God didn't comfort you so you'd be com-
fortable but so you could comfort others. One lady
told me she was able to get through her mastectomy
without falling apart because of other women who
came to her and provided living examples of how
they had made it through and were still smiling.

You may not need to go outside your church family to find others who are longing for encourage-
ment in the same area where you have suffered.

When you see the pathetic face and the open arms
of the next Cabbage Patch Doll, remember the people who need your help.

There is such a desire in human nature to belong
to somebody or some group who will give us some
collective identity. Many people join churches not
because of interest in spiritual things but because
they feel a need to belong. All of us want to know
we have a home. We want to know we have someone who will marry us and bury us. We want to
be part of a greater family; we want to be adopted
into the family of God even when we don't understand our own desires.

In Russia religious people are persecuted and kept
out of universities and government jobs, and yet
there is an unprecedented wave of spiritual zeal per-
vading the country. Even when we've been brain-
washed to turn from God there is that longing inside us that craves for a Savior.

What is your church doing to welcome people

warmly into the family of God? Do you greet guests each Sunday or assume that some committee will do it? Do you invite new people home for brunch or coffee, or do you feel that it's too much like work? There are so many lonely people who may look great on the outside but who are so empty inside. Fill them up with your love and attention.

How about your marriage? Do you really belong to each other? Have you adopted each other for better or for worse? Have you made a "till-death-do-us-part" commitment?

We never fight for something to which we are not committed. When it's a casual relationship we too easily opt for the exit. Spend some serious discussion time with your mate, and renew your deep and trusting commitment to each other.

From here on when you see a Cabbage Patch Doll complete with adoption papers, renew your own commitment and ask the Lord to make you aware of those lonesome people who want to belong to the family of God.

7

Especially for Teens

Even if you teens have not read the beginning of this book, you all know that the Cabbage Patch Kid is the sensation of the century. In the previous chapters I have reviewed the "birth" of this baby and shared with the readers why this particular doll has caught on: Each one is guaranteed to be unique, all are pitifully in need of mothers, and they are not purchased, but adopted. I have explained that I have my own Cabbage Patch Doll, my 21-year-old son Frederick Jeffery. He is a unique creation, born of two young people who should never have gotten together in the first place. He was put into a foster home at birth and was in need of a real mother. My husband and I took this baby and adopted him.

When our Fred was 16, he had a friend who got a girl pregnant. The boy married her, divorced her, and left his own child. Why did Fred's friend abandon his son? He left because he wanted to avoid the responsibility that accompanies childbirth. He made love to this teenage girl as casually as taking her to the movies. He had no thought of commitment; he just wanted a good time. She probably thought that in order to be popular this was expected. Neither one meant to get in trouble, but now here's an adorable little boy who will grow up knowing he was rejected by his father and assuming, as he grows older, that his mother wasn't too thrilled with his birth either. It's hard enough to bring up well-adjusted children in a warm and loving home environment, but how difficult when rejection is inevitable fact!

For you teenagers reading this, what lesson is there from out of the Cabbage Patch? Let me review a few of your current excuses for free love without commitment.

It will never happen to me. With all the birth control devices and pills with all the printed matter on the subject, there are still hundreds of thousands of teenage pregnancies each year. There are still mistakes; things somehow go wrong. My sister-in-law once took in unwed mothers for the duration of their terms. Every one of them told her, "I never thought it would happen to me." A statistic was headlined in the *New York Times*, "Unwed Mothers Account for 37% of New York Births."[54] In 1964 it was 11 percent; in 1973, 25.6 percent; and now 37 percent. With all the information available and the sex classes in high school, teenage pregnancies are rapidly rising, and no loose lover can assume, "It will never happen to me."

Girls: never believe any young man who tells you, "You have nothing to worry about," "I know when

to stop," or, "If you really loved me, you couldn't
say no."

Young men: never count on "I'm on the pill," or
"It's okay this time of the month."

If these comments were always true we wouldn't
have 37 percent of the New York births as illegiti-
mate babies, nor would the welfare rolls be so high.
Fully 45 percent of the New York women who
receive Aid to Families of Dependent Children
became parents in their teens, and even worse is the
fact that this is a self-perpetuating problem.

> Children born out of wedlock tend to have
> children of their own out of wedlock.

> There is a definite linkage between juve-
> nile delinquency and children raised with-
> out fathers.

> Children of unwed mothers were also
> more likely to be abused.[55]

In the August 1984 *Ladies Home Journal* was an
article titled "Contraception, The Hope That Failed."
It told that when "the pill" came out in 1960, women
felt their troubles were over. Yet in a recent survey
in which 92 percent of the women between the ages
of 15 and 44 said they used contraceptives, the con-
clusion was, "Our record of effective use is abysmal.
Today, almost a quarter of a century later, we are
back to square one. Out of every two pregnancies,
one is still unplanned."[56]

With all the scientific advantages and information
available, mistakes still occur.

Teenagers do get pregnant. It can happen to you!

I can always have an abortion. In today's free society it is legal to have abortions, but just because the
state gives license to scoff at God's laws does not

mean that they have found ways to wipe out the
guilt that accompanies the willful destruction of a
human life. I have talked to too many young girls
who have taken this option and years later still have
a resident black cloud traveling overhead. Some
have never been able to have a child later, a disap-
pointment enlarged by the memory of their choice.
Some have told me they thought it would be a simple procedure quickly forgotten, but they cried
throughout, realizing the seriousness of what they
were doing. Not one was able to dismiss it lightly.

A psychiatrist told me that a large portion of people in mental hospitals today are there because they
have a guilty conscience they can't release over some
mistake they made many years ago.

Some young girls, in fear of their parents finding
out, resort to self-abortions. They rely on methods
told them by other teens who think it worked for
someone else: purposely falling down stairs, jump-
ing off high ladders or the porch roof, or doing
what's called "coat-hanger surgery." Every year
many girls die needlessly because they have tried
to abort a pregnancy themselves or gone through
an illegal operation by some unskilled person who
left them to die.

Some teens resort to drugs, pills, or potions they've
heard about. One told me she took doses of castor
oil because she had once heard her mother say of
a lady who had too many children, "She should have
taken castor oil." What the mother meant we'll
never know, but the girl ended up in the hospital
in agony but still pregnant.

My mother can take care of the baby. That is surely
a possibility, and I've listened to those mothers who
thought they were through with child-raising only
to have their daughter's baby thrust upon them.

Natural instinct causes a grandmother to love the child, but there is often an open war with the child's parent. The young mother wants to be mother in name but wants to get out of the house as quickly as possible and back to her schooling or other activities. The grandmother resents the drastic changes in her life and the daily responsibility without authority. Probably the grandma and grandpa have differing opinions on whether the baby should live there in the first place, and if so, how much of their routine must be rearranged. Frequently a three-way fight ensues, and this is further complicated if the young father is on the scene.

With Fred's friend, he lived with the girl's parents. The mother couldn't stand the sight of him because she felt he had "done in" her daughter. The father hated him, and the boy in turn didn't like either of the girl's parents. The girl was tossed about among them and divorce was the ultimate solution, leaving them all emotionally drained and disturbed.

One friend my age was "given" two children by her daughter. She has raised them since they were little, but at various times when the real mother felt a burst of responsibility she would appear, snatch the two from her mother, and take them to some apartment for a few days or a week. She would fill them with negatives about the grandmother and then, when she tired of baby-sitting, she would drop them off on the doorstep. This went on for years and kept the children unstable and fearful. The children have never quite known who they were or where they might end up.

Another lovely lady I know has cared for her grandchild since birth. The irresponsible mother went off to do her own thing, ending up in jail for drug-trafficking. From her cell she wrote soulful letters to her child telling her she would come and rescue her from the "bad grandmother" when she got out. The child, who had lived a relatively stress-free life, began to have nightmares, became emotionally upset, and is mixed up about whether she wants to be "rescued" or not.

You can sometimes dump the baby on another person, but you are ensuring the development of an emotionally unstable child who will have a love-hate relationship with you. It is not fair to your mother or the child to bestow responsibility on someone else and yet retain the ultimate parental authority for yourself if and when you feel like exerting it.

Don't use your mother's understanding nature as a backup excuse for promiscuity.

We can always get married if we have to. How lightly teenagers take the easy option of getting married "if we have to"! One lady told me that she "had to get married." She did her best to make a harmonious home, but every morning when she awoke, her first thought was, "He would never have married me if he hadn't been forced to." In case she ever forgot, he often reminded her of the fact. Twenty miserable years and five children later they got divorced.

In-law relationships may be a problem in any marriage, but difficulties, even animosities, are ensured if the wedding is "under the gun." Each set of parents holds hostilities toward the other family, especially the unrelated bride or groom. With statistics saying that at least one out of two marriages will end in divorce, what chance is there for a couple who "had to get married"? She blames him for getting her pregnant and he blames her for ruining his life.

Those who blithely say "We can always get married" just as casually say "We can always get divorced."

While magazines and TV make this uncoupling seem simple, I've never known anyone who found going through a divorce an easy experience. No matter how cool you might try to be about it, each of you would say things to each other that would produce lasting damage. Even after a loveless marriage, divorce inflicts the pains of rejection.

An attractive 40-year-old-woman told me she had to get married at 15. She was a mother at 16 and felt totally cheated out of her youth. She meant to be a good mother, but she deeply resented this little girl who had prevented her from enjoying her teen years. When the girl was 16, she repeated her mother's mistake and got pregnant herself. The mother gave up on the daughter and on her own husband and got divorced. As she talked to me, she was living alone and taking lessons in tennis and horseback, trying to make up for the teenage years she had never had and for the 25 years she felt she had wasted.

Marriage should not be an institution you flee to when you get caught, but a uniting of two mature adults who are in love and excited about committing their lives to each other "till death do us part." That expression may sound old-fashioned, but any other reason for marriage will be doomed to failure.

I can always leave town. "If worse comes to worst," a sexually active teen told me, "I can always leave town and nobody will ever know." How simple it sounds to run away from our problems, and how often many of us have tried to avoid the consequences of our actions! Seldom are we successful, no matter what the seriousness of our situation may be, but in pregnancy the problem is physically car-

ried along with the person. There's no running
away and leaving it behind.

I met two attractive pregnant girls at *Jesus North-
west*, where I had just spoken. They were Christians,
Sunday school teachers, good girls. Each had taken
"one chance." Unfortunately, one chance was one
too many. They came from distant sections of the
state and didn't know each other, but each one had
been advised by a mother or pastor to "leave town."
They had both come to Portland, Oregon, and both
started attending the same church. One said, "You
have no idea how people's attitudes change when
they find out that you're pregnant and there's no
husband. We were the only two unwed mothers-
to-be in the adult Sunday school class, and we really
felt ostracized by the rest. Finally we quit going, and
now we pal around together waiting out our time."

Later this girl wrote me a letter and said her friend
was so homesick that she had returned to her
mother, who agreed to see her through the pregnancy in spite of the stigma attached to it in the community. The girl who wrote was then in her eighth
month. She was both toxic and ill with a lasting
pneumonia, as well as lonely and depressed. She told
me she had called the local church when she desperately needed medicine and food and couldn't get
out of bed to go to the store. A lady had done her
errands but told her the church would not help her
again "because after all you got yourself into this
predicament, and besides, you're not even a mem-
ber."

Leaving town is always a possibility, but how
lonely to have a baby with no one around who cares!
How depressing to go through a difficult delivery
and not even have a baby to take home! That's what
happened to this girl who was sick through it all,

had no support from family or church, and who gave up the baby for adoption.

I can give the baby up for adoption. Having been on the receiving end of this statement, I am very grateful for the young mother who provided me with an exceptional son, yet she must often wonder where he is and what has become of him. On his birthday I know she must think of him, for she had "left town" and delivered him alone, knowing she would never see him again after his birth. Giving a baby up for adoption may be the best of several poor choices, but it's so much better to have never gotten pregnant in the first place.

One Sunday morning in a motel I turned on the TV to a well-known pastor and was fascinated with his announcement of a home for unwed mothers sponsored by his church. He told of the plight of these teens who have to make major decisions in life, often in faraway towns while lonely and depressed, and who later may regret their choice. He was starting this home to provide a loving Christian environment for the unfortunate girl and to offer intelligent and objective counsel for her in her time of need. For those couples wanting to adopt a baby, his staff would make this service available. I was blessed by this announcement, but saddened by its necessity.

What can be done with all these teenage pregnancies? The world says, "Have more classes on sex, provide free birth-control clinics, make abortions more easily available, expand Aid to Dependent Mothers." The solutions never seem to include teaching God's simple truth of reserving sex for marriage! We read nothing advising teens not to engage in sex—only articles on how to use contraceptives or how to abort an unwanted baby. The *New York Times* admits that the city is troubled by all of these out-of-wedlock babies, but amazingly they said their concern is "not for moral reasons" but because it's costing the city too much in "increased spending for welfare, day care, police, and other social services." The experts also add, "Children raised by unmarried mothers are more likely to lead lives of poverty and to have a harder time educating themselves, finding work, and assuming adult responsibilities."[57]

After belaboring the problem with no practical answers to this costly situation, the article quotes Eleanor Holmes Norton, a professor at Georgetown University who is in favor of a program that would teach school children about the lifelong consequences of teenage pregnancy rather than simply emphasizing birth control or abortion.[58]

Sociologist Dr. Kenneth Clark says, "Someone has to reach out to these young people, and someone would have to consider them worth the effort required—and it would not be easy."[59]

It would not be easy to bring young people back into some kind of moral standing, but there are some of us who have seen the damage done physically and emotionally to teens who didn't mean to get in trouble and yet who did. I feel it's worth the effort to keep trying and to attack the problem at its source.

Senator Jeremiah Denton of Alabama is the author of The Adolescent Family Life Bill, enacted into law in 1981. This bill encourages chastity and seeks to help pregnant teenagers release their babies for adoption or decide to keep them. Denton says:

> I think we have an obligation in terms of human happiness to try to delay until marriage and continue within marriage the exclusivity of sex. If you stop trying to do

that, you have both personal and national disaster."[60]

Some of you may not want solutions that curtail your free lifestyle. Some of you teens may feel you've been preached at for years by your parents or the pastor. So let me, an objective woman whose life will not personally be affected by your decisions, share with you that casual teenage sex will leave all of you with feelings of guilt that will not float away. It may also leave some of you with choices you should not have to make at this stage of life, choices which can drastically change your whole future. You may end up married to someone you don't even care for and find yourself a parent when you can't even support yourself. You may one day discover yourself alone and estranged from your family, with emotional and financial supports removed when you need them most. You may end up making hamburgers in McDonald's when you had planned to be a doctor. You may never get the education your mind deserves because you decided to show your parents you could do your own thing and get away with it. You did it, but you didn't get away with it. Some of you may give up a child for adoption and spend the rest of your life wondering where he is, crying on his birthday, longing for him on Christmas, looking for him in every crowd. "Love 'em and leave 'em" is not as simple as it sounds.

God is not against sex; He invented it. But He intended it to be between two people who are committed to each other through marriage, two who are mature enough to be responsible parents.

In Brooklyn, New York, there is a neighborhood project called *Teens in Crisis* that is designed to deal with the unwed teenage father, the frequently forgotten partner in this rampant social problem. The Director, Anette Guardo, tells in the *New York Times* that at first "they're very pleased to be poppas, and initially they have a kind of false bravado. They see the child as a vehicle for adult status. They think, 'I'll be a father; somebody will love me and need me.' But they haven't weighed the responsibilities of parenthood, and that's where our project comes in."[61]

Maturity means responsibility and commitment, so grow up and don't say:

It will never happen to me!
  —For it might.

I can always have an abortion.
  —The results can range from guilt to death.

My mother can take care of the baby.
  —Responsibility without authority leads to troubled relationships.

We can always get married if we have to.
  —With full knowledge that most forced marriages end in divorce and rejection.

I can always leave town.
  —And feel left out, lonely, and depressed.

I can give the baby up for adoption.
  —And spend the rest of my life wondering where he is.

Let's be realistic and put aside these irresponsible excuses.

Leave the production of Cabbage Patch Kids—all

unique, in need, and adoptable—to Coleco Industries, which turns out engaging babies who don't need to be fed, trained, or sent to college.

It may sound old-fashioned in today's free-love society, but God will not be mocked and we do reap what we sow. Don't take any chances; don't leave in your Cabbage Patch a unique baby, in need of a home, to be picked, adopted, and raised by somebody else. It is vital to our well-being to know how God views each person—

- unique
- special
- one-of-a-kind.

NOTES

1. *Newsweek*, Dec. 12, 1983.
2. Ibid.
3. Ibid.
4. Ibid.
5. *San Bernardino Sun*, Dec. 23, 1983.
6. *American Way*, Feb. 1984.
7. *Waco Tribune-Herald*, Jan. 27, 1984.
8. *San Bernardino Sun*, July 23, 1984.
9. *New York Times* News Service.
10. *Waco Tribune-Herald*, Jan. 22, 1984.
11. Proverbs 22:1.
12. Ecclesiastes 7:1.
13. Acts 6:3.
14. Acts 10:22.
15. Acts 16:2.
16. Acts 22:12.
17. 3 John 12.
18. Isaiah 56:5.
19. Genesis 2:18 NIV.
20. *Waco Tribune-Herald*, Jan. 22, 1984.
21. *Newsweek*, Dec. 12, 1983.
22. Ibid.
23. Ibid.
24. Ibid.
25. Ibid.
26. Matthew 26:11 NIV.
27. Deuteronomy 15:11.
28. Psalm 82:3.
29. Acts 20:35.
30. Deuteronomy 7:6,8.
31. Psalm 6:2,6-9.
32. John 1:12.
33. Romans 8:15,16 TEV.

34. Ephesians 2:19 TEV.
35. John 3:16.
36. 2 Corinthians 5:17.
37. Ephesians 4:24.
38. Isaiah 62:2.
39. Matthew 28:20.
40. Ephesians 1:13,14 TEV.
41. John 3:16.
42. Genesis 48:5,16.
43. Exodus 2:10.
44. Esther 2:7.
45. Genesis 48:16.
46. Isaiah 40:1.
47. *Time*, Apr. 9, 1984.
48. Ibid.
49. Ibid.
50. Ibid.
51. Ibid.
52. 2 Timothy 1:12.
53. *Time*, Apr. 9, 1954.
54. *New York Times*, Aug. 13, 1984.
55. Ibid.
56. *Ladies Home Journal*, Aug. 1984.
57. *New York Times*, Aug. 13, 1984.
58. Ibid.
59. Ibid.
60. *New York Times*, Aug. 20, 1984.
61. Ibid.